THE ABERYSTWYTH CLIFF RAILWAY QUIZ BOOK

A Comprehensive Guide to Constitution Hill's Victorian Marvel

INTRODUCTION

Welcome to the definitive quiz book about one of Wales' most beloved attractions - the Aberystwyth Cliff Railway on Constitution Hill. This funicular railway has been carrying passengers up the scenic hillside since the Victorian era, offering breathtaking views across Cardigan Bay and serving as a testament to ingenious 19th-century engineering.

Whether you're a local enthusiast, a railway buff, or simply curious about this remarkable piece of Welsh heritage, these questions will test your knowledge of everything from its construction and operation to its cultural significance and technical specifications.

A BRIEF HISTORY OF THE ABERYSTWYTH CLIFF RAILWAY

The story of the Aberystwyth Cliff Railway begins in the bustling Victorian era of the 1890s, when seaside resorts across Britain were experiencing unprecedented growth and innovation. The railway emerged from the ambitious vision of the Aberystwyth Improvement Company, which sought to transform the Welsh coastal town into a premier spa resort destination rivalling the fashionable watering holes of England.

The Visionary Beginning (1895-1896)

In 1895, the Aberystwyth Improvement Company commissioned the brilliant engineer George Croydon Marks to design what would become one of Britain's most enduring tourist attractions. Marks, who had begun his career as an apprentice at Woolwich Arsenal in 1871 and later studied at King's College, brought both technical expertise and innovative thinking to the project. His background in military engineering and his partnership with publisher Sir George Newnes provided the perfect combination of technical skill and financial backing.

The construction of the railway presented formidable challenges. Constitution Hill's steep gradient required the excavation of over 1,200 tonnes of rock to create a suitable route. The track had to be laid in a deep cutting that required concrete stabilisation, and four footbridges were constructed to maintain existing pathways that crossed the new railway line. Despite these obstacles, the engineering team completed the 778-foot track in remarkable time, creating what was then the longest electric cliff railway in Britain.

The Grand Opening and Victorian Heyday (1896-1920)

The Aberystwyth Cliff Railway officially opened to the public in 1896, immediately capturing the imagination of Victorian tourists. The original system employed an ingenious water balance mechanism that exemplified Victorian engineering creativity. One carriage would have its water tank filled at the summit whilst the other was emptied at the bottom station, creating the counterbalance needed to operate the system safely and efficiently.

The railway was an instant success, carrying visitors to the summit where they could enjoy the spectacular Camera Obscura and breathtaking views across Cardigan Bay. The hilltop attractions formed part of what was essentially Britain's first theme park, complete with various Victorian leisure facilities that made Constitution Hill a must-visit destination.

George Croydon Marks' design proved so successful that he went on to create similar railways, including the famous Lynton and Lynmouth Cliff Railway in Devon. His work established the template for British funicular railways, with three other railways built to his basic design.

Modernisation and Electrification (1921-1950)

The year 1921 marked a pivotal moment in the railway's history with the introduction of electrification. The charming but labour-intensive water balance system was replaced by a reliable electric motor, though the fundamental counterbalanced carriage system remained unchanged. This modernisation ensured the railway could operate more efficiently whilst maintaining its essential character.

The electrification represented more than just a technical upgrade; it symbolised the railway's transition from Victorian novelty to essential piece of transport infrastructure. The new system proved its worth through the challenging decades that followed, including two world wars and changing patterns of British tourism.

Post-War Recognition and Heritage Status (1950-1987)

The post-war era saw growing appreciation for Victorian engineering achievements, and the Aberystwyth Cliff Railway began to be recognised not merely as a tourist attraction but as an important piece of industrial heritage. The railway's robust construction and thoughtful design had enabled it to operate continuously for decades, proving the quality and durability of Victorian engineering.

This recognition culminated in November 1987 when the railway was granted Grade II listed status, formally acknowledging its architectural and historical importance. The listing recognised not only the technical achievement but also the railway's cultural significance as part of Aberystwyth's identity and Wales' industrial heritage.

Modern Era and Charitable Stewardship (1987-Present)

Today, the Aberystwyth Cliff Railway operates under charitable trust management, ensuring its preservation for future generations whilst maintaining its role as a vital tourist attraction. The railway has been carefully modernised to meet contemporary accessibility requirements, becoming fully wheelchair accessible whilst preserving its historic character.

Modern safety systems have been integrated with the original mechanical principles, and the carriages continue to tilt to keep passengers level during their gentle 4mph journey to the summit. The railway now serves not only tourists seeking spectacular views but also diners visiting the hilltop restaurant and visitors to the Camera Obscura.

Engineering Legacy

At 237 metres in length, the railway holds the distinction of being the second longest funicular railway in the British Isles, surpassed only by its sister railway at Lynton and Lynmouth. The sophisticated electronic safety systems now supporting the high-tensile steel cables represent the evolution of Victorian mechanical ingenuity into the digital age.

The railway's continued success demonstrates the timeless appeal of well-designed public transport. Its tilted carriages, carefully engineered passing loop at the midpoint, and spectacular coastal setting continue to enchant visitors more than 125 years after George Croydon Marks first envisioned its route up Constitution Hill.

Cultural Impact

The Aberystwyth Cliff Railway has become more than mere transport; it represents the enduring appeal of Victorian innovation and the successful marriage of engineering achievement with natural beauty. Local residents affectionately call Constitution Hill "Y Consti," reflecting the railway's integration into the community's daily life and identity.

As both a working piece of transport infrastructure and a cherished heritage attraction, the railway embodies the successful preservation of industrial history. It continues to carry thousands of passengers annually, each journey retracing the path first carved through rock and vision by Victorian engineers whose work remains as relevant and appealing today as it was in Queen Victoria's golden jubilee year.

The Aberystwyth Cliff Railway stands as a testament to the enduring power of thoughtful engineering, community stewardship, and the timeless human desire to reach great heights whilst enjoying spectacular views. Its story continues to unfold with each gentle journey up Constitution Hill, carrying new generations of visitors into its remarkable legacy.

SECTION 1: HISTORICAL FOUNDATIONS

1. In what year did the Aberystwyth Cliff Railway first open to the public?

Answer: 1896

2. Which company was responsible for developing the Cliff Railway as part of the Constitution Hill project?

Answer: The Aberystwyth Improvement Company

3. The railway was formed in which year, one year before it opened?

Answer: 1895

4. What was the primary purpose behind the creation of the Cliff Railway?

Answer: It was developed to take visitors to the top of Constitution Hill where various Victorian attractions were established, as part of making Aberystwyth into a desirable spa resort

5. What significant change occurred to the railway's power system in 1921?

Answer: The railway was electrified, changing from its original water balance system

6. What was the railway's original operating system before electrification?

Answer: A water balance system, where one carriage had its water tank filled at the top whilst the other was emptied at the bottom

SECTION 2: ENGINEERING AND DESIGN

7. Who was the brilliant engineer responsible for designing the Cliff Railway?

Answer: George Croydon Marks

8. What notable political position did George Croydon Marks later achieve?

Answer: He became Lord Marks, a Liberal peer, and served as a Cornish MP

9. Where did George Croydon Marks begin his engineering career?

Answer: He commenced his apprenticeship in the Royal Laboratory Department at Woolwich Arsenal in 1871

10. What is the total length of the Cliff Railway track?

Answer: 778 feet (237 metres)

11. Where does the Aberystwyth Cliff Railway rank amongst British funicular railways by length?

Answer: It is the second longest funicular railway in the British Isles

12. Which railway holds the record as the longest funicular railway in the British Isles?

Answer: The Lynton and Lynmouth Cliff Railway in Devon

13. What speed do the carriages travel at during their journey?

Answer: 4 miles per hour

14. How much rock had to be excavated during construction?

Answer: 1,200 tonnes (though some sources mention 12,000 tons in the mid-section cutting)

15. How many footbridges were constructed to accommodate existing paths that crossed the railway cutting?

Answer: Four footbridges

16. What unique feature distinguishes the railway's carriages from conventional train cars?

Answer: The carriages are tilted to remain level as they traverse the inclined track

17. What safety system supports the high-tensile steel cables?

Answer: A sophisticated electronic safety system

SECTION 3: TECHNICAL SPECIFICATIONS AND OPERATIONS

18. What is the gauge of the Cliff Railway track?

Answer: This is a narrow gauge railway

19. How are the two carriages connected?

Answer:They are connected by a cable in a balanced system

20. What powers the modern railway system?

Answer: A powerful electric motor

21. Why was most of the track constructed in a deep cutting?

Answer: The cutting was necessary due to the terrain and had to be stabilised using concrete

22. What makes the railway fully accessible to all visitors?

Answer: It is fully wheelchair accessible

23. Are pets permitted on the railway?

Answer: Yes, it is dog-friendly

24. Approximately how long does a complete journey take, including loading and unloading?

Answer: About 10 minutes

SECTION 4: HERITAGE AND RECOGNITION

25. When was the Aberystwyth Cliff Railway granted Grade II listed status?

Answer: November 1987

26. What organisation currently operates the railway?

Answer: A charitable trust

27. How many other railways in the UK were built to the same basic design as the Aberystwyth Cliff Railway?

Answer: Three others (the Clifton Rocks Railway in Bristol, the Lynton and Lynmouth Cliff Railway in Devon, and the Bridgnorth Cliff Railway)

SECTION 5: CONSTITUTION HILL ATTRACTIONS

28. What popular Victorian attraction sits at the very summit of Constitution Hill?

Answer: The Camera Obscura

29. What does the Camera Obscura feature that provides views of the surrounding area?

Answer: A fourteen-inch lens that reflects an all-round view of the town and surrounding countryside

30. What modern attraction was erected on Constitution Hill for Millennium celebrations?

Answer: A beacon, which was lit on 31st December 1999 as part of 1,300 beacons across the country

31. What type of dining establishment operates at the summit?

Answer: A fine dining restaurant and café

32. What spectacular natural feature can visitors enjoy from the top of Constitution Hill?

Answer: Breathtaking views across Cardigan Bay

SECTION 6: VISITOR EXPERIENCE AND MODERN OPERATIONS

33. What special offer is available to visitors who gift aid their ticket?

Answer: A free ride on a second day

34. How can visitors access the lower station of the railway?

Answer: By walking along the seafront and then making a short climb to the bottom station

35. What should visitors expect during busy periods?

Answer: They may need to queue as the journey takes about 10 minutes including loading and unloading

36. What affectionate local nickname is given to Constitution Hill?

Answer: "Y Consti"

37. What time of day can visitors enjoy the restaurant facilities at the summit?

Answer: Day or night - it operates for both daytime visits and evening dining

SECTION 7: GEOGRAPHIC AND LOCATION QUESTIONS

38. In which Welsh county is the Aberystwyth Cliff Railway located?

Answer: Ceredigion

39. What body of water provides the scenic backdrop for views from Constitution Hill?

Answer: Cardigan Bay

40. What is the relationship between Constitution Hill and the town of Aberystwyth?

Answer: Constitution Hill sits at the edge of the town

SECTION 8: CONSTRUCTION CHALLENGES AND SOLUTIONS

41. Why was concrete necessary during the railway's construction?

Answer: To stabilise the track that had to be laid in a deep cutting

42. What infrastructure was required to maintain existing foot traffic during construction?

Answer: Bridges had to be constructed to carry footpaths over the cutting

43. What geological challenge did the construction team face?

Answer: The need to excavate substantial amounts of rock from the hillside

SECTION 9: RAILWAY CLASSIFICATION AND COMPARISONS

44. What type of railway system is the Aberystwyth Cliff Railway technically classified as?

Answer: A funicular railway

45. How does a funicular railway system work?

Answer: It uses two balanced carriages connected by a cable, with one carriage counterbalancing the other

46. What was innovative about the railway when it first opened in 1896?

Answer: It was the longest electric cliff railway in Britain at the time

SECTION 10: VICTORIAN TOURISM AND DEVELOPMENT

47. What type of development was Constitution Hill intended to represent in the 1890s?

Answer: A Victorian leisure venture and early theme park

48. What was the Aberystwyth Improvement Company's vision for the town?

Answer: To transform Aberystwyth into a desirable spa resort

49. How did the railway contribute to tourism development in Victorian Aberystwyth?

Answer: It provided easy access to hilltop attractions, stimulating the development of Constitution Hill as a leisure area

50. What era of engineering innovation does the Cliff Railway represent?

Answer: Victorian engineering, showcasing the ingenuity and ambition of 1890s construction techniques

SECTION 11: MODERN RECOGNITION AND TOURISM

51. What type of events can be hosted at the summit facilities?

Answer: Business and social events, as well as fine dining experiences

52. How has the railway adapted to modern accessibility requirements?

Answer: It has been made fully wheelchair accessible whilst maintaining its historic character

53. What role does the railway play in contemporary Aberystwyth tourism?

Answer: It serves as a major tourist attraction offering scenic transport to hilltop attractions and dining

SECTION 12: ENGINEERING LEGACY

54. What other major railway project was George Croydon Marks involved with?

Answer: The Lynton and Lynmouth Cliff Railway in Devon

55. What educational background did George Croydon Marks have?

Answer: He was educated at the Royal Arsenal School, Woolwich, and later studied engineering at King's College after obtaining a Whitworth Exhibition

56. What does the continued operation of the railway demonstrate about Victorian engineering?

Answer: The durability and quality of Victorian engineering, as the railway has operated successfully for over 125 years

SECTION 13: SEASONAL AND WEATHER CONSIDERATIONS

57. During which seasons is the railway typically most popular with visitors?

Answer: The railway operates year-round, but is particularly popular during the warmer months when the views are clearest

58. What weather conditions provide the best experience for railway passengers?

Answer: Clear days when the views across Cardigan Bay are unobstructed

SECTION 14: CULTURAL SIGNIFICANCE

59. What does the railway represent in terms of Welsh industrial heritage?

Answer: It represents an important example of Victorian transport engineering and tourism development in Wales

60. How has the railway contributed to Aberystwyth's identity as a seaside resort?

Answer: It has been a defining feature of the town's tourist appeal for over a century, providing iconic hilltop access

SECTION 15: TECHNICAL TRIVIA AND INTERESTING FACTS

61. What happens when one carriage reaches the top while the other reaches the bottom?

Answer: They pass each other at the midpoint of the journey in a carefully engineered passing loop

62. What was the original method for controlling the water balance system?

Answer: Water tanks were filled at the top station and emptied at the bottom station to create the counterbalance

63. Why are the carriages tilted rather than remaining parallel to the track?

Answer: The tilt ensures passengers remain level and comfortable during the inclined journey

64. What maintenance challenges does the railway face due to its coastal location?

Answer: Exposure to salt air and coastal weather requires regular maintenance of metal components

65. How has the safety system evolved since the railway's Victorian origins?

Answer: Modern electronic safety systems have been added while maintaining the basic mechanical principles

BONUS QUESTIONS - EXPERT LEVEL

66. What was the approximate cost of the original construction in 1896?

Answer: Historical records would need to be consulted for exact figures, but it represented a significant Victorian investment

67. How many passengers can the railway typically carry per hour during peak operation?

Answer: This depends on carriage capacity and the 10-minute journey time including loading

68. What other attractions were originally planned for Constitution Hill alongside the Camera Obscura?

Answer: Various Victorian leisure attractions were part of the original development plan

69. How has the railway survived major historical events such as both World Wars?

Answer: It has maintained operation through significant historical periods, demonstrating its importance to the local community

70. What role did Sir George Newnes play in funicular railway development?

Answer: He was George Croydon Marks' business partner and provided financing for railway projects

CONCLUSION

The Aberystwyth Cliff Railway stands as a remarkable testament to Victorian engineering ingenuity and the enduring appeal of well-designed public transport. From its water-balanced beginnings to its modern electric operation, this Grade II listed railway continues to enchant visitors with its unique tilted carriages and spectacular coastal views.

Whether you scored perfectly on every question or learned something new about this Welsh treasure, the railway itself remains the best classroom for understanding its rich history and continued significance. Next time you ride the gentle incline to Constitution Hill's summit, you'll appreciate not just the views across Cardigan Bay, but the remarkable story of vision, engineering, and perseverance that makes the journey possible.

Visit the Aberystwyth Cliff Railway and experience this piece of living history for yourself!

Quiz Statistics:

- Total Questions: 70
- Categories: 15 themed sections
- Difficulty Levels: Beginner to Expert
- Focus Areas: History, Engineering, Operations, Tourism, Heritage

Thank you for testing your knowledge of the Aberystwyth Cliff Railway!

Discover the Secrets of Wales' Most Beloved Railway

For over 125 years, the Aberystwyth Cliff Railway has been carrying passengers up Constitution Hill, but how much do you really know about this Victorian marvel? From its ingenious water-balanced beginnings to its modern electric operation, this remarkable funicular railway holds countless fascinating stories waiting to be discovered.

Inside this comprehensive quiz book, you'll explore:

• The brilliant engineering mind of George Croydon Marks and his revolutionary design • Victorian tourism ventures that transformed Aberystwyth into a premier resort destination
• Technical marvels including tilted carriages, counterbalanced systems, and safety innovations • Construction challenges that required excavating over 1,200 tonnes of rock • The railway's Grade II listed heritage status and cultural significance to Wales • Modern accessibility features that preserve history whilst serving today's visitors

Whether you're a local resident, railway enthusiast, or curious tourist, these 70 carefully crafted questions will challenge and delight. From basic historical facts to expert-level engineering trivia, discover why this second-longest funicular railway in the British Isles continues to enchant visitors with every gentle 4mph journey to the summit.

Perfect for railway buffs, Welsh heritage lovers, quiz enthusiasts, and anyone who's ever marvelled at the spectacular views from Constitution Hill. Test your knowledge, learn fascinating facts, and gain a deeper appreciation for one of Aberystwyth's most treasured attractions.

"More than just a quiz book – it's a celebration of Victorian ingenuity and Welsh heritage."

Climb aboard the pages and discover the remarkable story behind every journey up Constitution Hill.

Printed in Dunstable, United Kingdom